Ben's Adventures

🐚 A Day at the Beach

Written by
Elizabeth Gerlach

Illustration by yip jar

To my babies ~
Ava, Colin and sweet Benjamin, my angel.
We miss you, my beautiful boy.
Fly free on your next adventure.

CharleyHouse Press, LLC.

Text and illustrations copyright by Elizabeth Gerlach 2018

All Rights Reserved.

No part of this publication, may be reproduced in whole or in part, stored in a retrieval system, or transmitted in any way, or distributed in any form or by any means without prior written consent from the publisher.

ISBN: 978-1-7327034-0-7

All inquiries, comments or questions on this book can be submitted to author Elizabeth Gerlach at www.Bens-Adventures.com

Printed in the United States.

Hi, my name is

Ben.

This is my family.

I have Cerebral Palsy and use a wheelchair.

And, I am a triplet with a brother AND a sister.

I am soooo lucky!

I can't walk.

I can't talk.

But that's okay!

I use my imagination every day.

Today I'm dreaming about the beach.

I feel the sun on my face, the breeze in my hair, the sand at my feet. And I smile from my chair!

One, two, three, I count...
but the crabs are too fast!

WATCH OUT FOR THE WAVES, I say!
So many crabs running for cover.
They hide in the sand until the wave is over.

"Let's build a sand castle," I say to my friend.

He says, "Sounds good!"

We make our plan.

With one tower built and two more to go...

I kick and laugh

and then think, "OH NO!!!"

My friend thinks it's funny.
I'm glad he's not mad.
He says, "No worries.
We'll make a NEW plan!"

The beach is my playground,

it's where I'm carefree.

I run around and I can be me.

I love—sand on my toes...

the sweet air in my nose,

the bright blue of the sky

and the sea gulls that fly!

I dream of daddy's kite.
He has it down the beach.
It's so—so high, so very high!
It's almost out of reach.
"Ben," he yells, "you wanna fly?"
And I respond, "Yes, please!"

He loves to fly the kite
with me and my big brother.
We take turns again and again.
Does he ever tire, I wonder?

I dream I'm with the kite.

I'm high and so free...

bobbing and bouncing in the clouds.

You can too, if you believe!

Along the shore we look for shells,

just me and Colin and Ava.

We'll keep them in our bucket—

all the blue, pink, white and silver.

We'll wash them off,
and put them away.
Then pull them out,
to remember this day.

Time to head home,

our beach day is done.

The sights, sounds and feelings

all become one.

I will keep them locked away

to remember this day.

This time together, we adore,

and how we just wish...that we had more.

AHHH...I'm back home and tucked in my bed.

"Hi, sweet boy. How was your day?" Mommy asks.

I want to tell her—"I took us to the beach!"

But instead, I drift off to sleep and wonder about tomorrow's adventure!

Benjamin Robert Gerlach loved being outside with the sun on his face and the wind in his hair. He was a triplet, brother, son, friend, student and churchgoer. He was also a young boy living with cerebral palsy and epilepsy. But this didn't define him! He loved toys, noises, movement, his preschool class, his brother and sister, and his mommy and daddy. He had many challenges in his short life but lived each day with a smile on his face. After a two-year fight with multiple respiratory illnesses, Ben lost his battle on May 2, 2016. This book is dedicated to Benjamin with great hope that it shows that everyone deserves to have an adventure. And despite physical or medical differences, all kids can play and dream!

Elizabeth Gerlach lives outside of Chicago with her husband, Rob, and Ben's brother, Colin, and sister, Ava. In Benjamin's memory, they have created the **Ben Smiles Memorial Foundation** to spread smiles in Ben's name by giving gifts of adapted/accessible toys and other small devices to kids with fine and gross motor challenges from **Ben's Toy Closet**, and by performing various community service projects through **Ben's Team**.

A portion of book sales will benefit

www.BenSmiles.org